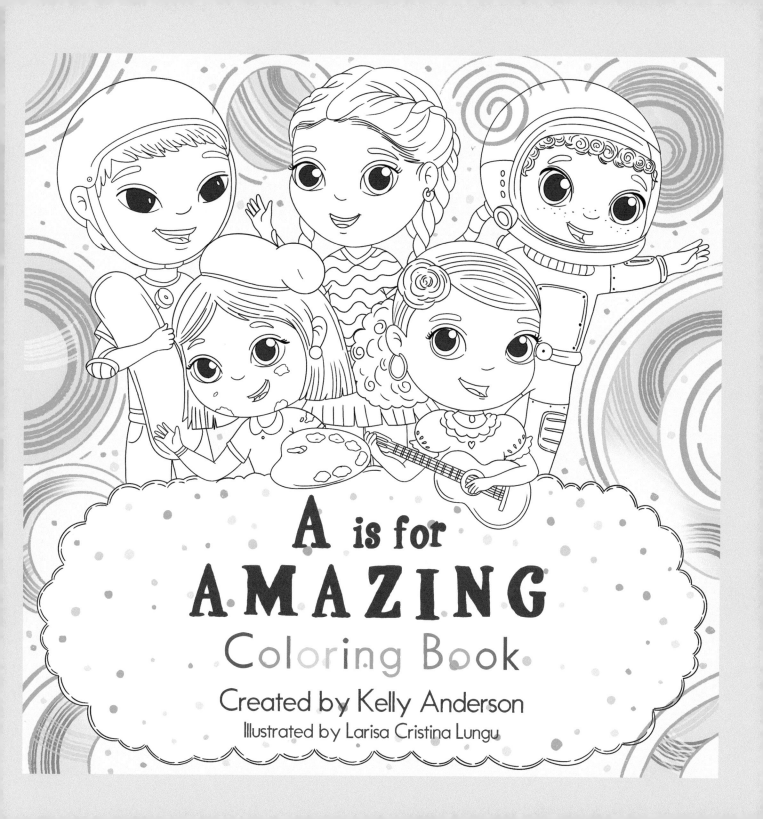

A is for
AMAZING
Coloring Book

Created by Kelly Anderson
Illustrated by Larisa Cristina Lungu

Archway Publishing books may be ordered through booksellers or by contacting:

Archway Publishing
1663 Liberty Drive
Bloomington, IN 47403
www.archwaypublishing.com
844-669-3957

ISBN: 978-1-6657-2605-4 (sc)
ISBN: 978-1-6657-2604-7 (e)

Print information available on the last page.

Archway Publishing rev. date: 08/02/2022

ARCHWAY
PUBLISHING

ADVENTUROUS

BRILLIANT

CREATIVE

DYNAMIC

ELEGANT

FEARLESS

GENEROUS

HELPFUL

IMAGINATIVE

JOYFUL

KIND-HEARTED

LIFE SAVER

MEGASTAR

NEIGHBORLY

ORGANIZED

PRICELESS

QUALIFIED

RESPONSIBLE

SPECTACULAR

TEAM PLAYER

UNSTOPPABLE

VOGUE

WELL-MANNERED

ZANY

Printed in the United States
by Baker & Taylor Publisher Services